Leading Character

Also by Dan B. Allender

LEADING CHARACTER

DAN B. ALLENDER

WILLOW
Willow Creek Resources

ZONDERVAN.com/
AUTHORTRACKER
follow your favorite authors

 **ZONDERVAN®**

Leading Character
Copyright © 2008 by Dan B. Allender

Requests for information should be addressed to:
Zondervan, *Grand Rapids, Michigan 49530*

Library of Congress Cataloging-in-Publication Data

Allender, Dan B.
    Leading character / Dan Allender.
      p. cm. — (Leadership library)
    ISBN 978-0-310-28762-9 (hardcover, printed)
    1. Leadership—Religious aspects—Christianity. 2. Character—Religious aspects—
Christianity. I. Title.
    BV4597.53.L43A44 2008
    253—dc22   2008019094

Interior design by CHANGE Design Group

Printed in the United States of America

08 09 10 11 12 13 14 • 10 9 8 7 6 5 4 3 2 1

LEADERSHIP LIBRARY

The purpose of the Leadership Library is to provide leaders in all arenas—churches, businesses, schools, or nonprofits—with the cutting-edge thinking and the practical advice they need to take their leadership skills to the next level.

Books in the Leadership Library reflect the wisdom and experience of proven leaders who offer big insights in a pocket-size package. Whether you read these books on your own or with a group of colleagues, the Leadership Library presents critical insight into today's leadership challenges.

Leading Character

How did you first become a leader? Do you remember the circumstances? Maybe you earned an actual title to indicate you were the person in charge—the captain of the team, a candidate for public office, the CEO. Perhaps other people gravitated toward you naturally, counting on you for decisions and willingly following your lead. Or it's even possible that your leap into leadership resembled mine—and came about more or less as a matter of default.

I was teaching at Mars Hill Graduate School, which was, at that time, a satellite school of Western Seminary in Portland, Oregon. We were, however, in the process of moving the school toward independence, and six of us who were on the faculty were involved in this transition. At one point, about three years into the process, we were required to complete and sign an accreditation document. And one of the blanks on that form required an answer to this question: Who is the president?

I'll never forget that meeting. When it got to the point where someone had to consent to list their name as the president, the room got very quiet. As we looked around at one another, it became clear no one was going to speak. We were all testing each other, waiting to see who would be foolish enough to agree to such a thing.

Eventually, we reached a consensus that because I was the oldest, I would take on that position—although no one, including me, expected that I would ever really act as the president.

That assumption continued until the moment when, about four months later, we faced our first dismissal of an employee. And with that responsibility, I may have become the only human being in history ever to fire the same person three times in less than twenty-four hours.

I fired him, providing due cause and asking him to think and pray about our conversation. At the end of our forty-five minutes of interaction, I said we would speak again the next day, never imagining he would go home and create an entire plan as to how he could enhance his performance and revise his job description. He came back eager for the opportunity to present his plan—and it was clear the firing had not taken effect.

I gathered enough wisdom and strength to fire him again. At that juncture, he asked, because of certain things he was doing, if he could stay another week to ten days to finish those projects. I considered that an enormously gracious suggestion on his part. "How reasonable," I thought. So he went back to work.

Later that day, our receptionist—who had previously worked for a large corporation—asked me, "Is he still employed?" "Yes," I said, "but just for another week to ten days."

At that point, she began to enumerate all the things this person had access to and explained how this could be very problematic if he harbored any kind of ill spirit toward the school. Well, I hadn't even thought of an ill spirit, much less the complications that could occur. She told me that in her previous job, when employees were asked to leave, the company allowed them an hour or so to go to their desks and gather all of their personal belongings. Then they were escorted out of the building.

It made sense! Which meant I had to fire him for the third time.

And that was only the beginning. In the years that followed, I made every classic mistake a leader can possibly make. Then I invented some I don't believe ever before existed on the face of the earth.

But every mistake became a lesson learned. And very often these hard-earned lessons prompted valuable conversations with other leaders. I began to see that certain patterns surround outstanding leadership. I noted, for example, how often the leaders I most admired are each widely known for their strong, highly regarded character. That is not to say that they are stodgy, unimaginative, play-it-by-the-book kinds of people. In fact, most are quite honest about their struggles in ministry and with the wars of leadership.

Yes, they have impeccable integrity, but they also make me laugh. They not only wow me with their individuality and spontaneity, they impress me with their meticulous honesty and forthrightness. They struggle and worry about their kids. While they are committed to their marriages, at times they feel lonely and need more support from their spouses. They are real, human, fully alive, and beautiful people.

Too often, leaders suppress such openness. What they are allowed to say from the platform or in conversations with others is narrowed down to the "expected and tolerated," and all else must be hidden or denied. Such limitations create a degree of being two-faced—one face public, the other private.

At times that hypocrisy is even internalized. When this happens—when we deny the parts of ourselves that would cause disruption if they were seen or acknowledged in polite company—we are on shaky ground. Because no one can live long with such disparity without a loss of integrity.

We are to *have* a
character that invites others
to see the goodness of Christ
and to *be* a character that intrigues
and compels others to discover what
it means to be forgiven and set free
to live with passion and joy.

No one is immune to the public-private face war.
Sometimes the face we present in public requires immense
courage; other times, the public face is an indication of great
cowardice. Are you aware of when you have been courageous
or cowardly? I pray that by reading and then reflecting on
this material you will be encouraged to consider both
possibilities.

Eventually, I came to realize that leadership is all about
character. And that the Christian leader, no matter what
he or she oversees, has the opportunity to be a *leading*

character—an example, a living representation of the power of the resurrection and the privilege of the fellowship created by sharing in Christ's suffering.

We demonstrate what it means to be a "leading character" by living this reality before those who are part of our organizations. We communicate our vision and strategies, we support and affirm our employees, we strengthen successful programs, we scrap processes that are no longer effective, and far, far more. But never should we do these things without making Christ known through word and deed. The primary focus is not what we speak, but how we live. We are to *have* a character that invites others to see the goodness of Christ and to *be* a character that intrigues and compels others to discover what it means to be forgiven and set free to live with passion and joy.

In short, the most effective leaders invariably embrace two fundamentals in this regard:

- The first is to *have* a character.

- The second is to *be* a character.

HAVE A CHARACTER

Say the word *character* and a dozen associations come to mind. There are character witnesses and character actors. We live in a culture all too familiar with character assassination. And we're intuitively aware of whether the behavior displayed by someone we know is "in character" or "out of character."

Primarily, though, we associate the presence of character with virtues, including honesty, courage, and truthfulness. Few compliments are more valued than to be regarded as a person of outstanding character. Everyone would agree that a leader's character is a key component of a leader's effectiveness.

Our character reflects our creator. We are made in the image of God, and the nature of God's personhood is woven into the deepest fabric of our being. To understand our character, we must begin with a glimpse of God's character.

God's Character

Since every human being—the believer and the unbeliever—is made in God's image, we all bear a character that *reveals* God. What does it mean for us to reveal God in our personhood, through our personality, and through our character? One of the most concise ways to sum up this very nature of God is found in Psalm 62: "One thing God has spoken, two things I have heard: that you, O God, are strong, and that you, O Lord, are loving" (vv. 11–12). In a few words, the psalmist captures the essence of God's character—*strong* and *loving.*

God's strength is absolute and is in no way dependent on anyone or anything outside of the Godhead. God is fully God, lacking nothing. God is also love, and he has chosen to bind himself with loyal covenantal passion to his creatures. God is free and bound, independent and utterly committed.

How can both of these be true? Many would argue that if God is strong, he can't also be loving—since so much suffering exists in the world and he has done nothing, apparently, to end it. Such logic further suggests that if God is loving, then he can't be strong, since God's love would then be predicated on his power. But the conundrum is ours, not God's. God is both strong and loving, and this presents no contradiction or conflict for the Trinity.

God's strength is reflected in his sovereign authority over all that exists and all that transpires. Nothing happens that is a surprise or out of his control. He has authority because he is the author. And while he is not the author of sin, he uses even that to accomplish his sovereign purposes. Look at God's boast to Job:

> Who shut up the sea behind doors
>> when it burst forth from the womb,
>
> when I made the clouds its garment
>> and wrapped it in thick darkness,
>
> when I fixed limits for it
>> and set its doors and bars in place,
>
> when I said, "This far you may come and no farther;
>> here is where your proud waves halt"?
>
> —Job 38:8–11

God's creative power and ordering of the world is part of his strength. His strength is also demonstrated by the boundaries he set for how we are to live, and both his law and the consequences for transgression reside under his authority. The fullness of his power, however, cannot be cataloged and understood; it can only be honored with awe and obeyed with reverence.

Yet, God is more than power; God is love. Scripture is filled with comparisons and descriptions meant to help us grasp the depth and inclusiveness of God's holy and never-ending love for us. That love is compared to the tender compassion of a mother for her child, for instance, and God is portrayed as bending his knee to whisper kindness to encourage his child's faint heart. We are told God's love seeks us even in the angst of longing and hurt, and we are frequently reminded of his mercy and loving protection. As is the case with his power, the fullness of God's love cannot be cataloged and understood; it can only be honored with gratitude and offered to others in reverence.

God uses his strength and love for honorable and wise purposes. He is fiercely loving and tender to his people. And we have been made to reflect God's character in all of our relationships.

Our Character

The actual word in the Greek—*charaktér*—originally was used in connection with tools designed for engraving. And character is indeed a tool that marks us—that in one sense cuts us, shapes us, and engraves us. We are image-bearers who are intended by God to make him known in a fashion that no one else on the earth can do in the same way.

Our marking is as unique as a snowflake. From a distance we all look reasonably alike, yet upon closer scrutiny our engraving is phenomenally distinct. Each person is engraved with a marking—face, body, parents, intellect, birth order, talents, passion, burden, and calling—that is different from any other human being. Our character is a complex interaction between God's writing of our body and background, the contributions others make to our life, and our unique participation in cowriting our story with God. The totality is our character, how our "marking" appears to others.

In Greek philosophy, character became a list of virtues that were considered requisite of a good citizen. You can see how the word then came to mean our reputation and, eventually, how it began to represent a series of virtues that one must desire and work to attain. If one lacked these virtues, then one had a bad character; if one succeeded, then one possessed a good character.

As simple as this seems, it must be underscored that the gospel compels us to live out a paradox: The more progress we make, the more we need grace. The more righteous we become, in fact, the more we are aware of how deeply we are flawed and how much we need forgiveness. Character development—described as a simple increase in virtue—is not, therefore, a Christian concept.

To better understand our character and how it affects the organizations we lead, we must see how God has marked us, how sin has marred us, and how God has chosen to remake us in the image of Christ.

We Are Marked

The nature of our character is our marking—and because we are made in God's image, every one of us has the marking of God's glory. So how are we to use those attributes of God's glory? What are we instructed to do as a result of being made like God?

The two attributes that reveal the glory of God—that show the marking, or character, of God in our lives—are the same two the psalmist uses to describe God's character (Psalm 62:11–12). We reveal the very character of God—in our lives and in our leadership—when we are strong and when we are loving. Being made in God's image, God has given us the capacity to move with strength and to do so with a tender heart.

Soon after God names our identity in Genesis 1:26, he also establishes our calling, providing us with opportunities to demonstrate these God-given attributes. "Then God blessed them and said, 'Be fruitful and multiply. Fill the earth and govern it. Reign over the fish in the sea, the birds in the sky, and all the animals that scurry along the ground'" (Genesis 1:28 NLT).

This passage is often referred to as the "cultural mandate," the belief that we are to apply God's principles to all aspects of society. It implies that all people—male and female, at all times and in all cultures—are called to the same standards as a result of being God's image-bearers. It would be far too simplistic to say that we are called to make babies and farm, although these are both valid examples of our mandate.

To give birth and cultivate growth require immense strength and tenderness. We quickly learn that to be true as we live out the first aspect of the cultural mandate by launching a new business, planting a church, developing a medical breakthrough, or taking any idea through the slow process from gestation to birth. Strength and tenderness are crucial as we "tend the garden," whether we're streamlining a process, training employees, negotiating with integrity, or discipling new believers. (You can see why the Great

We reveal the very character of God—in our lives and in our leadership—when we are strong and when we are loving.

Commission is widely regarded as Jesus' version of the cultural mandate.)

If one neglects any aspect of God's character, then neither birthing nor growing will go as God intended. Sadly, many leaders are gifted with great strength but choose to ignore tenderness. Too often, leaders are unwilling to be tender because it appears to lessen their authority or control over others. Other leaders are far more tender than strong and carefully avoid conflict with their colleagues or senior leaders. We all tend to champion one element of God's character and to excuse ourselves for ignoring or denying the other.

Let me offer an example: A friend whose daughter was diagnosed with leukemia didn't want to burden his company's employees with his personal suffering. He was deeply respected as an efficient and fair boss, but was seen as somewhat aloof and distant. As he dealt with his daughter's illness, his work became chaotic. No one had a clue as to what was going on—except for the fact he was changing before their eyes.

Learning of his problems at work, I asked him what troubled him about sharing his story with the employees. He said, "I don't want them to pity me or be watching over my shoulder." I told him that instead of pity, he was creating confusion, and even though he did not want to be watched over, that's exactly what was taking place as suspicions grew. We forget that people always watch leaders to gauge the security of their world.

Subsequently, my friend opened his heart in a company-wide meeting. He admitted that he had failed to be as tender to their daily struggles as he was now asking them to be on his behalf. The response of his company was sincere sorrow, relief, and even greater commitment. His strength had created great respect, but his absence of tenderness had created a more distant workplace. Once he allowed this tragedy to open his heart, the culture of his company improved.

Some leaders are great at providing creative vision to begin a work but are miserable at growing and maintaining movement in an organization. Others are phenomenal at supporting growth but terrified at starting something new. Seldom is this a matter of right or wrong; more often it reflects the differences in our calling and giftedness. Yet, when starters lack tenderness and maintainers lack strength, it is far more than a matter of giftedness and calling. It is a flight from growing more in the character of God.

Take a deep breath and, with pen and paper in hand, answer two questions:

- Do people at work see me as more tender than strong, or more strong than tender?

- What are the obstacles or risks involved in change?

Your strengths in one or the other are to be admired. Do you thank God for those strengths? The area of your weakness is not merely to be changed; first, it must be pondered, reflected on, and opened before God for his input.

We are men and women who are *marked* to be both strong and tender. The complexity arises because we are also *marred* by sin (see Genesis 3).

We Are Marred

Sin distorts. It dulls and diminishes the vivid marks of God's image in our lives. It negatively impacts how the character of God is revealed through our strength and tenderness. When sin does its work, these qualities of strength and tenderness become so deeply bent and marred that we fail to reveal the markings we were intended to show. And when we are marred by sin, we fail to reveal the glory of God.

The consequences of our sin become a process of hiding and blaming, just as our original parents, Adam and Eve, did after they rebelled against God. Notice that Adam and Eve hid rather than gather the strength to cry out for mercy and tenderness. Instead of having the courage—the strength—to be exposed and to bear the consequences, Adam first blamed God for having created Eve and then blamed Eve for having given him the fruit. We too fail to humbly stand before God to seek his tender mercy; we too turn against God with revolting strength to pour contempt on him—and anyone else in our line of fire—when we are exposed.

Notice that the apostle Paul expresses strong concern regarding contempt for God's kindness. He asks, "Or do you show contempt for the riches of his kindness, tolerance and patience, not realizing that God's kindness leads you toward repentance?" (Romans 2:4).

Each one of us might want to stop here, for a moment, and thoughtfully answer Paul's question. Do I show contempt for the power of God's kindness? Have I forgotten that it is his tender love that draws my heart to repentance? Contempt belittles and mocks and allows us to turn away from something that unnerves us. Instead of demonstrating true strength, we too often resort to contempt. Rather than being tender and vulnerable, we flee and hide. These not only mar our character, they diminish the way we lead our organizations.

My dear friend and copresident at Mars Hill Graduate School, Ron Carucci, came into my office one day. He wasn't happy and, as he sat down, he said, "You have created a mess and I have spent the last several hours mopping it up."

I must preface the rest of the story by saying I do not question Ron's love and respect for me, but when he spoke, I immediately turned both sick and hard. I had no idea what I had done wrong and I hated to hear what was coming. Although the details are now fuzzy, my failure had been to begin micromanaging an event that already had been in process for several weeks.

As I listened to the details of my failure, I immediately began to justify in my mind what I had done. I had actually been immensely patient in a process that seemed poorly managed, I told myself, and had simply offered a few suggestions as to how it could be improved. In fact, I had been too busy (cowardly flight) to get involved, and my remarks (barely hidden contempt) were heard by those planning the event as undermining their authority.

Ron's intervention was strong and kind. I began fluctuating between skewering myself with contempt and blaming others for my failure. In a matter of mere seconds, my response was to quit—to withdraw and lick my wounds. But Ron also named that tendency of mine. He understands that if one starts surgery, it is wise not only to complete the surgery but to extract as soon as possible all the issues of flight and fight.

We talked and prayed. It became clear to me that I not only needed to apologize and address the discouragement I had caused but, going forward, I needed to find ways to get involved early in the projects that most affected me, rather than waiting until the superstructure had been built before trying to revise it.

How obvious! Well, it's obvious now, but at the time, no one had ever before addressed this issue with me. Instead, they had hidden while viewing me with contempt for this

A leader's failure is never isolated, involving only the leader. Usually the failure of a leader involves basic patterns of hiding and blaming throughout the whole organization, patterns that must be uprooted.

pattern of mine. A leader's failure is never isolated, involving only the leader. Usually the failure of a leader involves basic patterns of hiding and blaming throughout the whole organization, patterns that must be uprooted. But the solution must always begin with the senior leader. If the fix doesn't begin with the leader, then any efforts to address it in the so-called rank and file will be futile.

As a consequence of our being marred, when we risk the possibility of our weaknesses or faulty motives being exposed, we grab our fig leaves and run for the bushes. And when we are exposed, because the One who knows us seeks us out ("Where are you?" God called to Adam), our natural response is to blame someone else for our actions.

Perhaps one of the most revealing, severest, and cruelest remarks ever said to God was spoken by Adam in this accusatory phrase: "The woman you put here with me—she gave me some fruit from the tree." And then, almost in a whisper as an afterthought, he adds, "Okay. And I ate it." Is that ownership? Absolutely not. It's blaming. It is a way of saying, "I'll take responsibility only if another is at fault first."

We all can benefit by learning from Adam's (poor) example.

We need to seek the help of others to fully see and understand this problem of honesty and confession. I admit I am tragically blind. Without the eyes of those who see my refusal to take ownership for my failures, I will often name only a small portion of the cancer. It is often our most virulent critics and enemies who most want us to see our blindness—and who are only too willing to poke us in the eye to help us see better. Instead, go to a trusted friend, compatriot, or spouse who will tell you the truth with kindness and even tears. Ask them. Invite them. Persuade them to talk with you about your refusal to take responsibility for some ongoing failure in your life and your tendency to spread the blame to others. We are persons with both integrity and deceit. We must use our integrity to invite others to expose our deceit, our hiding and blaming.

We Are Remade

We are marked to reveal God's strength—and yet, because of sin, that strength often turns to harshness. We are marked to be tender—and yet, because of sin, we are often weak and willing to compromise. The glory of the gospel is that in spite of our failures, God has *remade* us in the image of Christ to offer a different kind of strength and tenderness. Paul says that we are new creations, new persons in Christ:

> *Either way, Christ's love controls us. Since we believe that Christ died for all, we also believe that we have all died to our old life. He died for everyone so that those who receive his new life will no longer live for themselves. Instead, they will live for Christ, who died and was raised for them. So we have stopped evaluating others from a human point of view. At one time we thought of Christ merely from a human point of view. How differently we know him now! This means that anyone who belongs to Christ has become a new person. The old life is gone; a new life has begun! And all of this is a gift from God, who brought us back to himself through Christ. And God has given us this task of reconciling people to him. For God was in Christ, reconciling the world to himself, no longer counting people's sins against them. And he gave us this wonderful message of reconciliation. So we are Christ's ambassadors; God is making his appeal through us. We speak for Christ when we plead, "Come back to God!"*

> —*2 Corinthians 5:14–20 NLT*

My old life—your old life—died in Christ's death. And a new heart has been birthed in us. We are being remade.

This new heart can grow to God's fullness of character. This new heart gives me new eyes to look at every human being, including myself, from the perspective of heaven; my viewpoint is no longer limited to life under the sun. This new life gives me the capacity to call all people, including myself, to be reconciled with Christ—through my appeal, through my life itself. And we need God's help to do that.

Paul gives us an extraordinary picture of the transformation of our identities as leaders who are marked, who are marred, and who are being remade:

> *I thank Christ Jesus our Lord, who has given me strength, that he considered me trustworthy, appointing me to his service. Even though I was once a blasphemer and a persecutor and a violent man, I was shown mercy because I acted in ignorance and unbelief. The grace of our Lord was poured out on me abundantly, along with the faith and love that are in Christ Jesus.*
>
> *—1 Timothy 1:12–14 TNIV*

I believe one of our
central callings is to stand
before the community of God
and the world and to say,
"I am the worst of
all sinners."

Then Paul pauses, asking for our attention by saying:
"Here is a trustworthy saying that deserves full acceptance"
(as if everything else he said wasn't!). What he's trying to tell
us here is, "Everything I've said to this point is very important,
but now listen very, very carefully to this part": "Christ Jesus
came into the world to save sinners—of whom I am the
worst" (1 Timothy 1:15 TNIV).

As leaders, what are we to be when we stand before
our congregations or our organizations? I believe one of our
central callings is to stand before the community of God and
the world and to say, in effect, as Paul did, "I am the worst of
all sinners." Or we could honor Paul's prior claim to that title

> What would it
> mean for you to reveal
> your true character as you
> stand before those
> you lead?

by saying, "I am the worst of all sinners, except one." (Unless, after I've told you more of my story, you would prefer to revise that to "except two." That way, you could claim to be the third worst sinner on the face of the earth.)

Paul claims there's not another human being—past, present, or future—who will ever live with more enmity toward God than he had. And part of the glory of the gospel is that this man, our apostle, the one who in many ways brought us the fullness of Scripture, is referring to himself when he says, earlier in this passage, that the "law is made not for the righteous but for lawbreakers and rebels, the ungodly and sinful, the unholy and irreligious" (1 Timothy 1:9).

Paul goes on to name the unrighteous. They're perverts, they're liars, they're thieves, they're perjurers. He even includes these descriptions—mother-killers and father-killers—not found in any of his other lists of grave sins.

After going through the list of abhorrent and wicked sins, he then describes himself: "I, your apostle, am the chief of all sinners; I am the worst of all." He is immensely strong in acknowledging his sin—he does not flee from the truth. He does not blame others or even himself. He is amazingly tender in confessing the wonder of being forgiven, and he acknowledges his profound need for Christ. Paul gives us a rare picture of a redeemed man who, in his role as the apostle to the Gentiles, is unafraid to make himself known to those he leads.

Extreme Makeovers

What would it mean for you to follow Paul's example and reveal your true character as you stand before those you lead? Most of us grew up believing that if we were to tell the truth, if people knew what was in our hearts. . . what had just passed through our minds. . . what we had been either leaning toward or falling into. . . those we lead would decide we have no right to be in charge.

We know more is required of us if we are to follow Paul as he follows Jesus. And that means a profound makeover of our character and our leadership. But before we get to that, we need to understand that our culture has already undergone an extreme makeover of its own.

Our Culture

Many, if not most, of today's leaders came into their positions in a world that was deeply influenced by *modernism*. Basically, that approach to life told us that there are linear answers—principles through which, if we simply apply step one, step two, step three, step four—one after the other—our problems can be solved. We will enjoy a leadership structure that works, we will achieve relief from depression, we will have a better marriage, and we will have thinner thighs in thirty days. As a result, we have become linear, principle-oriented, and simplistically driven, wanting answers to our problems so much more than we want the person of Jesus Christ.

We see this in literature on leadership and at conferences on leadership that offer their instruction in four, seven, or twelve steps. Here are four steps to resolve conflict in the workplace, seven steps to become your organization's most effective leader, twelve steps to develop strategies for growth of your organization. The difficulty is that although the material offered may be excellent and worthwhile, the "sales pitch" is based on the implied promise that results are only four or seven or twelve steps away—and those steps can be readily tackled and performed effectively. This is also true for advice of a more personal nature. Marriage series, for instance, have been marketed with descriptions like, "In one CD you will find more hope and change than from any other single hour in your life." That is overstatement. It is pandering. It is snake oil. If there was any time in our history most likely to endure such schlock, it was during the era of modernism. But, Toto, we're not in Kansas anymore.

The dilemma for anyone still steeped in a modernist mind-set is that our world has changed. We now live in a *postmodern* world that does not accept and will never embrace some of the core assumptions of the modernist promise that mere facts and linear progress are life-changing. As a result, many people today—especially younger people—don't trust us or our leadership.

Let me, once again, tap into the wisdom of my dear friend Ron Carucci, who wrote in his book *Leadership Divide* that many fear we are facing a dearth of leaders. In fact, Ron says there are many individuals who are dying to lead but refuse to lead in the manner they have witnessed as the norm. They balk at the job-takes-all-to-advance mentality of the modernist leaders they see and are far more committed to family and friends than the modernists. They view hierarchy as a bastion of privilege, not as a necessity for making decisions. In countless ways, emerging leaders are asking hard questions—and finding the answers from their elders sorely inadequate and not convincing.

This new postmodern world is profoundly fragmented; and with that fragmentation, severely insecure; and with that insecurity, very suspicious of leaders. People are so suspicious, in fact, that they're angry at virtually anything we as leaders say. Everything we say is eventually examined to gauge how sincere, how honest, and how true we really are in our positions of leadership.

Consequently, if we continue to live in a world where all we offer are step-by-step solutions—whether they be for conflicts among coworkers, or organizational failures, or marriage problems—we will never connect to the real issues with the wisdom that results when we apply strength and tenderness.

This new postmodern world is profoundly fragmented; and with that fragmentation, severely insecure; and with that insecurity, very suspicious of leaders.

What moved us beyond modernism into this postmodern era? The world we live in now knows there are no easy answers—no easy explanations for a Hiroshima, for a World Trade Center, for a Virginia Tech. We recently ended a century that had more holocausts and more people butchered than at any other time in human history. Not surprisingly, the general consensus is that easy answers don't work. We need to step up to our responsibility as passionately committed leaders to find answers to the complex problems we face by engaging in more complex thinking.

If we respond to the problems brought to us by those we lead—whether those questions are simple or global—by

We need to step up to our responsibility as passionately committed leaders to find answers to the complex problems we face by engaging in more complex thinking.

slapping them with a simplistic answer using the usual linear approach of two or three principles, we will have failed. We will have planted the seeds of disappointment that can grow into both suspicion and despair and a lack of trust in our leadership abilities. Maybe the person leaves with a gracious "Thank you, that was very helpful." But I promise you, too often they leave thinking that what we offered was trite and self-righteous and didn't solve the problem.

Changing our approach, however, can pose difficulties. I spoke to one pastor, after teaching on this topic at his church, who said, "I don't differ with much of what you've said, but if I talked like you do about your struggles with God, your family, and your work, I'd be looking for work the following week." After hearing a few of his stories, I agreed with him—his job would be finished. His church was led by a group of angry, defensive, aggressive men who would not tolerate any "psychobabble" or newfangled ideas—nothing, in fact, that would not have been preached in the same way that their fathers had heard it in the same church decades ago.

For this pastor, and maybe for you as well, there is real wisdom in going slow and introducing small steps of change when examining our failures as leaders and our struggles with God. Patience is often a calling that must be embraced over many decades of ministry, even though the Bible is utterly, almost embarrassingly, honest about the shortcomings of our leaders. Consider Abraham, Isaac and Jacob, Moses and David. All these individuals were flawed, and yet the Bible doesn't flinch in telling a portion of the real story of each of these leaders. If you're a pastor, perhaps just preaching from these passages honestly and well, without mentioning any part of your own story, might be a good place to begin. Even that, however, may be more than some congregations can bear. Such was the case with this pastor, a reality that prompted me to ask, "Are you so committed to staying that you refuse to engage in a personal extreme makeover?"

How do we bridge the gap between the two very different worlds that exist in our jobs and in our churches? How do we come to understand the thinking of the new leaders who are emerging in this postmodern world? We

As Christian leaders, we must see ourselves as having "leading character" that invites others to see the goodness of Christ in us.

listen. We listen to the differences in worldview expressed. We listen without giving advice or disagreeing with their opinions. For only through listening with honest curiosity, without critiquing, can we begin to understand.

Our Character

As Christian leaders, we must see ourselves as having "leading character" that invites others to see the goodness of Christ in us. We must develop a way of thinking about leadership that allows us to be strong, yet tender, and stand before our congregations and our organizations and say that, as president or manager or pastor, our primary task is to "live the gospel before you." We must fully acknowledge that our gifts and talents are from God and reflect God's glory and beauty.

It's all about character.

In addition, we must acknowledge our propensity to sin, perhaps with an admission like mine: "I'm a marred human being—one who is full of hiding and blaming." To go deeper into our faults, look to Jesus, who expands our understanding of sin by using the words *lust* and *anger* (Matthew 5:21–30). He knows that we all struggle with these dark reactions. Lust is any desire that has gone mad and become a demand. Though the word *lust* is most often associated with sexual desire, other desires—lust for power, money, recognition—can be equally consuming. And when our desire is thwarted, we direct our anger at anyone who stands in our way, anyone who prevents us from getting what we demand—that which we believe will satisfy our need. Jesus does not take these destructive reactions lightly; in fact, he goes on to say that anyone who lusts is an adulterer and the person who is angry is subject to the same punishment as a murderer (Matthew 5:21–22, 27–28).

Jesus' words seem to be hyperbole. I may struggle with lust, but I've never had an affair. I may be angry at times, but is that as bad as killing someone? The radical makeover of our character that must take place begins when we embrace the wonder of being forgiven—but to accept forgiveness, we must first admit our need for it. So it's important for me to be clear: It isn't that I used to be lustful and angry; I am lustful and angry today and need God's forgiveness.

You may recall that decades ago, when Jimmy Carter was running for the presidency, he was asked by a *Playboy* magazine interviewer if he felt he was better than other Americans because he was a Christian. He said, "No," and added that he had struggled with lust like any other person. The reporter made his confession the featured element of the story. Jimmy Carter was held up to ridicule and made out to be a fool. Within a month his approval rating dropped by 10 percentage points. But was he a fool? If he was, then he was a fool in the same way Paul commends that we all be fools for Christ (1 Corinthians 1:18–31).

For many reasons, President Jimmy Carter is a hero. He had the courage to tell the truth, weather the consequences, and lead in a manner that has been recognized again and again as a model of peacemaking strength and fierce tenderness. His example encourages us to ask ourselves: Will I be honest, with wisdom and propriety, wiser than a serpent and innocent as a dove? And will I be tender, with honor and discretion, like a birthing mother and a compassionate father?

What is true of me, I believe, is true of you. And that is, we struggle. We struggle with hiding and blaming, with lust and anger. And what do the Scriptures say about the nature of who we are as a result of the fact that we lust, not just sexually, but for power, for prestige. . . just for a day off? When God calls lust "adultery," and ranks anger (apart from the righteous anger in service of his glory) as serious as "murder," it isn't hyperbole. It is the gospel truth.

What is the truth for each one of us? It's easy to let our eyes pass over the words we read and quickly agree or disagree with their validity without stopping to ponder the application of those words to our lives. How do we apply the words of Jesus regarding lust and anger? How would you name your interaction with your neighbor this morning—a reflection of lust or anger? How about the strained conversation with your teenage son or daughter? The moment we allow these truths to get personal, we find it is harder to tell the truth—and harder to believe in the gospel.

An extreme makeover for our character begins, then, when we embrace the gospel truth—of being marred and remade—alive in the freedom and power of the resurrection. Paul says, "I want to know Christ and the power of his resurrection and the fellowship of sharing in his sufferings, becoming like him in his death, and so, somehow, to attain to the resurrection from the dead" (Philippians 3:10–11). We become radically new when we bless our gifts and how God has marked our face, our story, and our calling; grieve our failings and the consequences on those we love and serve; and glory in forgiveness and live out resurrection freedom and boldness. Let's consider specifically how that can reshape the way we lead others.

Our Leadership

To have character as a leader means that you can talk about all three of these realities—being marked, marred, and remade. You can do that in the pulpit, at a staff meeting, or with colleagues one-on-one. The language you use can fit the context, rather than be spoken in the typical vernacular of religion.

I remember being at a U2 concert where the opening songs began to address the hunger of the human heart (made in God's image); then the songs moved on to expose the fact that everyone is prejudiced and envious (marred); and finally they described the hunger for a love that was all-seeing and all-embracing (remade in love). There are always innovative and unpredictable ways to reinvigorate and recast the matters of the heart. And these contexts can play a huge role in the makeover of our leading character when we are willing to get knowledge, seek prayer, grow in wisdom, and live with freedom.

Get knowledge. Nothing is harder to get than feedback from those you lead. If feedback has not been sought before, people will be reluctant to tell you the truth. If it has been done before and the data was used against others or was ignored, then, even if that happened on someone else's watch, your battle for honest feedback will be fought on an uphill slope. Leaders never get enough data about themselves—or the data they get is on either the extreme positive or extreme negative. Seldom is the data rigorous, systematic, or usable.

One of the best ways to get data on how you're doing is to hire an outside firm to orchestrate an analyzable 360-degree survey that asks a significant population of your subordinates, peers, and those to whom you report to evaluate you on many levels. Usually, the data will be anonymous and coded to help you and your organization assess your strengths and weaknesses so that you can implement change.

Other valuable data can be acquired by requesting feedback from trusted associates, friends, and family members. But simply asking, "Would you give me some feedback about what it is like to be around me or to work with me?" will result in either stunned silence or information that's so watered down it is of no value.

Instead, you have the best chance of getting useful feedback if you start the conversation by owning up to negative information everyone already knows about you. In other words, tell the truth as far as you can see it and then invite more data in that realm. As an example, I once said to a group of leaders at Mars Hill Graduate School, "I know when we get into this topic, I tend to panic. And I know that when I panic, I want to reach a quick consensus and I cut off conversation. I am not aware of other ways I handle myself at times like this. Can you help me see myself better and see what effect my behavior has on you?"

The responses I got were not easy to hear, but I took notes and did my best to clarify what each person had to say. I owned up to my failures. In addition, I built in two or three behavioral markers—or indicators—that would help me and the group recognize any reoccurrence of the same behavior. And I assured my staff that although I didn't want to derail our work again, I knew that it was likely to happen.

In this way, we built plans for moving into and through my problematic behavior to a safe and productive conclusion. Doing so provided us with far more than resolution of a particular problem. It reminded us that living out the gospel, not the mere completion of a project, was the reason we had gathered.

Seek prayer. Changing the processes and techniques we use as leaders will not result in transformation—of our work worlds or of our lives. Our prime tool for a radical makeover is prayer. I have failed to apply this truth more often than I have failed in any other dimension of leadership. I simply have not breathed prayer as air, and nearly all of my most suffocating moments in leadership have come about because I didn't pray, didn't ask others to pray, or didn't listen to what prayer had to teach me. I suspect that this failure is much like facing the damage caused to oneself by smoking cigarettes and then having to ask the hard question: "Why did I allow myself to do something that I knew would harm me?"

My excuse was often, "I prayed, but I don't have the time to pray more." How often I wish I had taken more time to talk

> A transformed leader prays more desperately and more often than he or she ever did prior to experiencing a radical makeover.

with God—up-front time that might have helped me escape the hundreds of hours it took later to resolve a crisis. I'm not saying that prayer will keep you from dealing with leadership crises, but I know this: I have faced a number of heartaches that could have been avoided had I sought more prayer from wise men and women outside of my work. If I had, I would most likely have been called to name and deal with realities that I, instead, ignored.

I have violated (and still do, at times) what is an exceedingly obvious principle: "If you are too busy to pray, then you have even more reason to stop what you are doing and give yourself over to prayer." A transformed leader prays more desperately and more often than he or she ever did prior to experiencing a radical makeover.

Grow in wisdom. Obviously, not everything in our lives ought to be shared with our associates. While we embrace the attributes of honesty and transparency, we must do so with judgment and wisdom. I once heard about a leader who began his work in a church by sharing with the other three staff members that he often struggled with sexual lust. Within a month, a church secretary reported to the elders how uncomfortable she was working with him—not because of any inappropriate behavior, but because his revelation had created its own tension.

Disclosure takes time, restraint, and wisdom. First, we should share nothing about our lives unless it has first been vetted by the people most affected by our disclosure. Certainly, our best stories and examples often involve other people, but they are not worth telling if doing so creates heartache for these individuals. If I want to tell a story that involves my wife or children, for instance, I talk with them first. And I ask these two questions:

- Is my telling of the story true as you remember it?
- Do you feel reluctant for any reason for it to be told?

Growing in wisdom also involves understanding the implications of our disclosures in the larger context of our work. After the departure of one of our founders, I was asked by students and alumni why I had fired the person. I had not in fact fired the person, but to go into the story of this individual's departure required details that would not only violate confidentiality but also our state's personnel laws. The questions were nonstop. Explaining why I couldn't talk about the situation only created more mystery and demand to know. It was a nightmare!

Eventually, I was asked about my failure during this process, and I knew that to articulate even personal failure could become fodder for a lawsuit. The questions sent me into a flight of stonewalling. Rather than address (with ethical and legal wisdom) what could be addressed, I fled. I blamed the person who had departed, the state of Washington's personnel law, the legal system, and anyone else who happened to be lingering near the problem. In retrospect,

I see that I could have simply talked about how it feels to not be able to answer. I could have engaged those who had questions in terms of the deep demand in my soul to be believed (a form of lust) and the resentment (anger) attached to my realization that nothing I could do would be enough. What I learned—too late to apply to that situation—is that we can be wise and still name what is problematic in our hearts.

As radically transformed leaders, we open ourselves up to being an example of redemption—past, present, and future. Yet our calling is also to never let those we work with forget that we are all first made beautiful in God's image and then gloriously remade in Christ's image. If all we do is confess to being marred, then we have not disclosed the truest truths about our glory. Often I find honest leaders more willing to

> As radically transformed leaders, we open ourselves up to being an example of redemption—past, present, and future.

acknowledge their failures than to confess the beautiful new heart that beats in their chests. Instead, we must disclose glory, hiding and blaming, cowardice and cruelty, and the new heart that yearns for courage and kindness.

Are you aware of why you argue against allowing your heart to be known by those you serve? Sometimes it is wise to write all those reasons on a piece of paper in order to see what patterns emerge. One pattern that will be difficult to name, at least for most of us, is the pattern of excuses that revolve around our lust to be appreciated, cared for, and respected. Another involves the contempt and withdrawal related to our anger. Until you've decoded your arguments— the ones you are conscious of (and seem so reasonable) and the deeper, more close-to-the-bone justifications—it will be nearly impossible to consider a different course of life.

Live with freedom. Too often we lose our way and find ourselves exhausted and overwhelmed with our work. Somewhere along the line, we lost our first love and the deepest impulse for why we accepted the mantle of leadership. The good news is that a radical makeover is almost always accompanied by a taste of invigoration. We need to be reminded what it means to be forgiven and set free to live with passion and joy, to be called "beloved." Then, no matter how weary and discouraged I have become, I find my heart amazed and sweetened by the privilege of leading. I am no longer aware of the burden.

A question we should ask ourselves at regular intervals is: "Am I having fun?" That question is a simple way to enter the deeper question, "Am I living in the freedom of the resurrection?" And if our answer is "no," then before we change jobs, careers, ministries, or employees, we need to ask ourselves this follow-up question: "Do I know the freedom of being humbled and being lifted up (see James 4:7–10) and the joy of being poor, sad, gentle, hungry, merciful, pure, peaceful, and persecuted?" (see Matthew 5:3–11). Anyone who once again answers "no" can assume that his or her heart needs to be surprised again by the gospel.

Jesus says, "And the truth will set you free" (John 8:32). He said this to people who refused to acknowledge that he spoke the truth and, instead, accused him of being demon possessed. We often call Jesus the truth and name ourselves as his followers, and yet because the cost seems not only too severe but crazy, we refuse to live with the freedom he invites us to know. We are bound by the judgment of others; we fear the power of man more than we are grateful for the kindness of God. And so we, too, say to Jesus, "You ask me to be and to do something insane, out of the norm, and it will get me into trouble, and I don't believe in you enough to do it."

The gospel turns the world, including our own lives, upside down—which, of course, is truly right side up. Not only are we to live in freedom, but we are to offer our unique lives as an

We are to *be* a character who offers our unique story as a lens for others to better see the life of Jesus.

example, a picture, of the work of redemption. Not only do we *have* a character that is meant to grow more and more into the image of Jesus but we are to *be* a character who offers our unique story as a lens for others to better see the life of Jesus.

BE A CHARACTER

Once we are comfortable with what it means to have a character, the next task of a leader is to *be* a character—to be open to all the various ways God may choose to work through each of our lives.

In his elegant book on leadership, *Leading Minds*, Howard Gardner looks at how a widely diverse group of leaders—from Gandhi to Eleanor Roosevelt—led by telling stories. Their stories articulated the unnamed fears that kept them from moving forward to what they most desired, and they offered hope, invigorating others to risk creating a new world. Stories are not mere illustrations; they are the fire and blood that create the possibility of transformation. The stories that great leaders tell link the individual leader's story to the lives of those she or he serves.

Most people will not follow a leader whose life is disconnected from their own story. Think how often American politicians offer their story of humble beginnings and their status as Washington outsiders as a means to convey the promise they will bring change to the morass of politics. It is a tiresome spin that gets dismissed quickly, yet it still works well enough to secure the support of voters. Leaders, no matter what the context, must communicate their vision and plans for how they intend to journey to the desired outcome for those they serve. This can only be done well through story.

A close friend who started a financial loan business took thirty of his executives to the poverty- and violence-filled section of Montreal where he grew up in order to introduce them to the section of town that inspired his company's name. My friend, who has suffered the cruelty and mockery of many for the physical disabilities related to albinism, wanted his executives to see why he values and loves his community and what it taught him about life. He invited these men and women to see, smell, and taste both heartache and hope. In addition to telling his story, he enabled his executives to see why he so prizes honesty, integrity, commitment, and risk taking. Stories shape how we see ourselves and how we envision our calling in the place we work and serve.

Every leader, no matter what the context, is a storyteller. And in telling stories we become a character in the stories of others. This friend, who took his executives on a story journey, later invited them to reflect on and write about what had motivated them to make money. He asked them to consider what they fear, what they are meant to overcome, and how their current work might be the context in which they can grow as people and not merely secure their financial futures.

In sharing his story, he helped his executives reflect on their own stories. The loan company is committed to making money, yet the culture established by this leader also provides significant sums to those who work with the homeless. By introducing his executives to the homeless and offering a means of partnering with the passions of their own hearts to give back to their world, he has become a character in their stories. A leader must *be* a character to lead others to greater "leading character."

Some Real Characters

Being a character is as old as time, and the Bible is filled with stories about individuals who were only too human—real characters—and yet were used by God in powerful ways. As we acknowledged earlier, the Bible is not reluctant to tell the stories of highly flawed and, at times, outright ridiculously failed human beings. Consider the life and story of our father of faith, Abraham.

God calls Abram to leave his home and country without telling him why he is leaving or where he is going. He obeys God. Yet within the same chapter that describes his departure (Genesis 12), he lies and tells Pharaoh's representatives that his wife, Sarai, is really his sister. He gets them all in big trouble. God has promised that Abram will be the father of a mighty nation that will bless all people. Yet when pregnancy doesn't occur, he allows his wife to talk him into taking a concubine to bear his child. It is a disastrous choice, and, eventually, he has to run off his son Ishmael and Ishmael's mother, Hagar, to keep peace with his wife.

As Abraham and Sarah, bearing the new names given

them by God, age and get beyond the expected years of childbearing, God sends a messenger to tell them they will have a son. Abraham laughs and then Sarah mocks the news. After this, in another bizarre flight from the truth, Abraham goes back to an old lie and creates new havoc by telling King Abimelech that Sarah is his sister. In his defense to the king, he basically says, "Well, I figured this to be a godless place . . . besides she is my sister—we both have the same father, though different mothers—and I married her" (see Genesis 20:11–12).

Abraham *blames* Abimelech's kingdom and then *hides* behind a technical truth while obscuring the fact that he is married to Sarah. This is the father of our faith—not such a great lineage, we might think. Yet, he is God's chosen leader to establish the people of God, Israel, and to bless the earth. Go figure.

Was there no one more righteous than Abraham, or Jacob, or Moses, or David? Jacob was a deceiver; Moses lost his way to the Promised Land because of his anger; and the apple of God's eye, David, was an adulterer and a murderer. It gives me pause to wonder why God called *me* into leadership. But then, I've been known to be a character myself.

Gone Fishin'

I have been amazed at how God uses the various foibles of my human nature to work in and through me. In the spirit of transparency I've been advocating, let me tell a story to illustrate my point.

A number of years ago, I had the privilege of sitting at lunch with a good friend who looked directly at me in the midst of our conversation and uttered these words: "You concern me because you're a very boring man."

How was I supposed to respond to something like that? "Uh, pass the salt. I'll try to spice up my life for you."

What I actually said was, "What are you saying?"

"You work too much," he said.

When I pressed him about his concern, he responded, "You have no hobbies. You take no breaks. You have no Sabbath. You don't take time off."

"Well, what do you suggest?"

"I want to take you fishing."

Say, what? To me, fishing meant holding a pole with a line going into the water. That line has a little red and white bulb attached that sits on the top, while the rest of it hangs below with a hook that has something dead on the end of it. And you hold onto that, being as still and quiet as possible, while you wait for something to happen.

His concern was boredom? Personally, I'd rather be locked in a closet!

I expressed these concerns and he said, "No, no, no, you don't understand. I want to take you *fly*-fishing."

A Wade in the Water

Well, I'd seen the movie *A River Runs Through It*. I knew fly-fishing meant wading into water and swinging the line out and back, and I could picture the beauty of the water and the rocks that surround this activity. I figured I could try anything moral once, and so, yeah, I went fishing. And within the first few minutes, my friend had taught me some of the little basics—enough for me to know that this really was going to be fun.

I just moved the line back and forth, back and forth. But about the third time I had it back, as I began to go forward, it wouldn't budge. I turned around and my friend had this look of astonishment mixed with horror and pain. I had hooked him in the ear! And he was right—fly-fishing was not boring! I got to take the hook out and do a little surgery.

I got into fly-fishing; I *really* got into it. I bought all the gear. (I didn't realize how much I'd enjoy gear. Now I understand that gear is to men what jewelry is to women.) I began to look at magazines and think about things like rods, reels, and waders.

Montana Mayhem

Around the time that I began fly-fishing, I received an invitation to teach at a Bible conference in Montana—and if you know anything about Montana, you know it's Mecca for people who fly-fish. So when I got this invitation, my answer came quickly and easily. It didn't require prayer . . . it didn't require asking God's will . . . I just said, "Yes!" I even took the additional step of inviting my wife and my ten-year-old son Andrew to accompany me.

The first day we were there, I didn't have to teach. So about 8:00 p.m., I went into the water with a float tube and all my gear. I was so excited! It was dusk and the mountains were beautiful. This was a wonderful, exhilarating break to be able to fly-fish before I was to teach the next morning.

I walked into the water, and although the beauty surrounding me as the sun began to set was the center of my attention, I couldn't help but notice that there were many birds flying around me. I'm really not an outdoorsy-type person and I don't know much about ornithology, but still, the presence of these birds surprised me. I guess I thought they would be in bed by then.

But they were fully awake, flying very rapidly as they went right over me, up and around me. And I thought, "Gosh, these birds are unusual." Suddenly, I realized they weren't birds. They were bats! And I am *terrified* of bats!

I started using my rod as a tool to create what I would call a No-Fly Zone. And as I was swinging my rod about—let's see, how should I tell you this?—you know how you always hear that you cannot hit a bat? Well, it's not true. I hit a bat. And it dropped into the water just a few feet from me.

At that point, I was horrified because I'd actually smacked a bat into the water. Then, as it surfaced, there was this moment—this very *intense* moment—in which this bat and I looked right at each other. Although I can't speak bat language, I had the sense that the bat was looking at me and thinking something like, "Look! An island!" as it began to move in my direction.

Well, there I was in my float tube, trying to move away from this creature. But it could swim much faster than I could move. Okay, I'm not proud of what I'm about to describe, but I have to say. . . it was self-defense.

I whacked the bat!

The first whack didn't work, so I whacked it again and again because it kept coming and coming. So I kept hitting at it and finally—this is horrifying to admit—I drowned one of God's creatures.

By this time, I was completely panicked. I wanted *out* of there. But at that moment, all of a sudden, a fish that had been created from the foundation of the earth for this very moment came and took my fly!

You might think that would be exciting. But I didn't *want* to catch a fish; I just wanted out of that water. So I reeled in as fast as I could, with no thought of playing this fish. I wanted it *in* so I could get *out*.

I must also tell you that up to this point, all I had ever caught were trout—sweet, small, beautifully colored trout. As I pulled this fish up, it became clear this was no trout. It was a big, ugly gray fish, and its huge mouth was opened very wide. I was startled!

I don't like to touch fish, but I had to get that big fish off the hook. Again, I can't explain it, but I just had kind of a meltdown. I tried to shake the fish off the hook, but I couldn't. I wanted out of the water so badly that I began swinging the fish. In fact, I swung that fish so hard that eventually I . . . forgive me . . . I ripped off its lips, which sent it hurtling back into the water.

I was out of there in nothing flat. It was dark by then, and I hurried to the dock and climbed up. Then, as I was walking toward the shore with all my equipment, I noticed a figure sitting on a chair about fifty feet away, near the end of the dock. As I got closer, I could tell it was a man—an older gentleman—and I started hoping I could just walk by him quickly.

Let me interrupt this story with a word from our sponsor. It may seem like a terrible time to break into the narrative, but I want to make sure you remember what I've asked you to consider in this book. Why did I want to walk by quickly? I didn't want to be seen. I didn't want to speak. I didn't want to make face-to-face contact with this man. I knew he'd just witnessed the entire bat-drowning-fish-ripping fiasco—which meant I'd been exposed as a complete failure as a fisherman. All I wanted to do was hide. It's one thing to say you're the worst of all sinners in a dignified public setting; it's much worse to be caught looking foolish by a stranger.

If you were to survey the major stories in my life—how I came to know Jesus, went to seminary, met my wife, got into ministry, pursued my education, and became part of a new graduate school—you would see certain issues that mark my life thematically. I have stories of shame, odd coincidence, violence, cowardly flight, and surly fight, and stories of sweet

It's one thing to say you're the worst of all sinners in a dignified public setting; it's much worse to be caught looking foolish by a stranger.

redemption that bring hope to my heart. How have these stories shaped me, molded me, and engraved my character for ill and for good? How do I tell these stories? We must look diligently at how all our stories have marked us and ask God: "How am I to use this engraving for your glory—where am I to serve, whom am I to serve, and how am I to serve in order to follow the marking you have worked into my story?" Was I being sensitive when I fired that employee who needed three firing conversations? Somewhat, maybe. But I was far more committed to having that man like me, and to think positively of me, than I was to be clear, concise, and, in one sense, to honor him in the process. We hide. We blame.

And that's exactly what I wanted to do on that dock. But as I walked by this man, he reached up and grabbed my arm. Then he pulled me down close to his face, and said, "Son, I've been fishing for over fifty years. I want you to know I have never seen the likes of this. And I just wanted to thank you."

I'm usually a pretty good communicator, but I had no words for that gentleman. And for the next several days at the conference, I avoided him.

If you're a teacher or leader, you know what it is to be in front of an audience when someone is sitting there who doesn't like you, who has spoken words against you, who questions your leadership, who doubts your sincerity, who has questioned your character in ways that have caused you pain. You know what it is like to have someone in your world who, as you see them, provokes all the questions you have about yourself, about God, about your work, about your leadership. I don't know what you do in those situations, but here's what I do: I avoid them.

And for the rest of the conference, I did my best to avoid this man who had seen me in the water. He sat right in front when I taught, but I moved my eyes up and around him. At meals, I ate on the other side of the dining hall. For a few days, I managed to keep him at bay.

Each day of the conference, I took my son fishing for a couple hours right after lunch. For three days straight, we caught nothing.

On that third day, as we were coming in, getting the boat secured and all the equipment back to our cabin, the gentleman I'd been avoiding pursued me. I could see him coming, out of the corner of my eye, and I knew I couldn't get everything done quickly enough to flee—which would have been too obvious anyway, even for me. When he got to me, he said, "I see you've been taking your son out to catch fish."

"Yes, sir, I have."

"I noticed you've been taking him out between one and three-thirty each day."

"Yes, sir."

"Also noticed you haven't caught anything."

"Yes, sir."

"Do you know that fish don't usually bite between one and three-thirty?"

"No, sir, I didn't know that."

"You don't know much about fishing, do you?"

"No, sir, I don't."

"Do you want your boy to catch a fish?"

"Absolutely. Yes."

"Then what I want you to do is be out here at five-thirty tomorrow morning."

He gave me two good lures and told me a few specific places to fish, information I did not have and would not have had if he had not spoken into my life—if he had not, in his own way, been an angel of confrontation, of information, of exposure. Had he not, in some sense, entered what a marred reality I reveal about Jesus Christ, I would never have known what I was doing wrong.

Just One More Cast

The next morning, Andrew and I went out at five-thirty. We were so excited. I had a sense that today would finally be the day. We fished from five-thirty to seven-thirty, but neither of us caught a thing. I had told my wife we'd be back at eight o'clock, so about seven forty-five, I looked at my son and said, "We've gotta go. We've got to go in."

"Oh, Dad, please, just let me fish a little bit more."

My first thought, though I didn't voice it, was, *What for? What for!*

And, although this was not one of the most profound issues in the world, I was ticked at God. Ticked at the fact that he could divide the Red Sea, but he wouldn't provide my son with one lousy fish—just because he has a father who's incompetent and doesn't know how to fish or where to go or what to do. I was furious with God, and there was a part of me, at that moment, that hated hope. I hated the prospect of looking at my son, knowing how much he wanted to catch a fish, and knowing that it was not going to happen.

With that thought, I looked at him and said, "No, we need to go."

He looked at me plaintively and very quietly said, "Please, Dad, just one more time?"

Inside, I was raging. Nevertheless, I looked at my son and answered with words tempered by a message the Spirit of

God had, in just that instant, spoken to me: *Do you want to kill hope in him? Do you want to kill hope in your son as you've allowed it, in this moment, to be killed in you?*

I softened. Who knows how it occurred, but I softened. I looked at my son and I said, "No, Andrew, you cannot fish *one* more time. But you can fish *five* more."

He looked at me with that look, like, "Really?"

"Yes," I said. "Not four, not six, *five*."

The first cast went out. Then the second. And the third. With each cast I prayed, "Oh, Lord, please let him have a fish!" By the fourth cast, I was back to thinking, *Why should I hope? Yeah, you suckered me into dreaming for my son again. I hoped again—and my hopes were dashed.*

I turned away from my son and began to pull on the oars as Andrew threw his line out for the fifth time. All of a sudden he was yelling, "Dad! Stop!"

I turned around and saw that his pole was bent over. "Andrew, move your rod around a little bit."

As he moved the pole around, I could see there was no movement on the line. "You've snagged a log or you've got a boot," I said, "but you don't have a fish." I turned back to the oars, but a moment later he yelled again, "Dad, look!"

This time I saw that now the line was moving. His rod was bent and it was moving! For the next five or six minutes, Andrew fought to bring in his fish. Soon we could see that he didn't have a beautiful mountain trout—what he had on his line was a northern pike! (I don't know if you've ever seen a northern pike, but they look downright satanic!)

As he fought to reel in the fish, I could tell Andrew was getting tired. At one point I said to him, "Andrew, let me hold the rod, just for a moment."

He looked at me and, probably thinking of my bat meltdown, said, "Like you did the other night?" I didn't know whether to laugh or cry.

When he finally got the fish up next to the boat, he said, "Dad, grab it!"

I looked at him and said, "It's *your* fish." (Hey, turnaround is fair play.)

We got his fish off the hook and rowed back to shore. It was a phenomenal moment. It was probably one of the most important moments, ever, in my life as a father. Then, perhaps one of the most important moments in my son's life took place as we neared the shore, when he said, quietly, "Dad, we have a God, don't we?"

I looked at him. "Yeah. Yeah, we do."

Another moment passed and he looked up at me. "Dad, I know God's name."

I had never heard him talk about the name of God other than, of course, the Bible names he had learned as a kid. "What do you mean, Andrew?"

"I know God's name."

"What is his name for you?"

What he said was, "God's name is 'the God of the fifth cast.'"

About four months later, that translated for him into coming to know Jesus Christ as his Lord and Savior.

Now, as I write this story, more than a decade has passed. My son is a brilliant, almost supernatural fisherman. It would be wrong for me to leave the impression that from this memorable fishing trip on, life has been smooth for us. It hasn't been. He has struggled in his faith, at times, and has fought and distanced himself from his father. But I have not forgotten a significant moment of redemption for me, for him, and for us. Nor has he. When we each have lost hope again that God would be God, the story has served not merely as encouragement but as a warning: "Do not forget the Lord your God," and we have been called to return to the fish that God so kindly brought to the surface.

Leading Character

Where did Andrew's insight come from? My faithfulness in teaching? My faithfulness of making the Scriptures clear to him? In one sense, yes. But far more, it came, in many ways, in the midst of my own humiliation, my own exposure, and my own propensity to blame God and others. Do you see that it is in the midst of bearing God's mark, his character, and of being marred by our own sin (and being willing to name that for our world rather than hiding from it) that God not only works to redeem us, but he works through us to reach others?

> The more you tell the
> truth about yourself . . . the more
> effective your leadership will
> become, the more you will
> develop a true leading
> character.

Too often we think sharing our weaknesses will cause
us to lose respect. We think making our weaknesses known
will cause us to lose the honor to be able to proclaim the
Word of God in our congregations or our businesses. I no
longer believe that is true. Not today, in our postmodern
culture. What I do believe is the more you tell the truth about
yourself—appropriately, winsomely, age-appropriately, within
a context—the more effective your leadership will become,
the more you will develop a true leading character. The more
you tell of your own failure of character, the more God will
use that for his purposes.

Do you see the handiwork of God in your story? We may never fully understand why we were given an alcoholic father or a distant and angry mother. We may never fully see God's deepest desire for our suffering or our blessings, yet we are intended to bless God for how he has written our life for his glory. What would it mean for you to bless the parts of your story that bear sorrow and joy, death and life?

Let us become people who can confess we are sinners. And when we do, what will be the effect? What will be the results for each of us?

REVEALING GOD'S CHARACTER

Despite the fact that the movie *Chariots of Fire* is nearly three decades old, there is a scene that many people still know by heart. As I speak before groups of various size and makeup, I enjoy asking the question, "When Eric Liddell said, 'I believe God made me for a purpose, but he also made me fast. And when I run I feel his . . .' what did he say?" Members of the audience nearly always joyfully respond, "Pleasure!" People remember this line because, in many respects, it is the key message of the film; the object of God's delight was clear. We experience God's delight, God's pleasure, when we do what he created us to do.

What do you do that most gives you a sense of God's delight? What brings you delight? This is a question designed to move you closer to determining what unique aspects of your life contribute most to revealing God's character. If you're a leader, then I hope leading is close to the top of your list—otherwise, you likely will not thrive or perhaps even survive your leadership experience.

Several years ago, I sat with a friend at breakfast and we talked with some seriousness about our lives. This man is a generous, peaceful presence, and he is often invited to teach in wildly diverse settings. He hates conflict, but has had to stand against a leader who has turned against one of his dear friends.

God loves to use our strengths to get us into battle. In my friend's case, his peace-making skills are well known and the basis for his being invited to mediate a contentious situation. The mediation required him to enter into a conflict that he would have preferred to avoid. But while God uses our strengths to get us into battle, he also uses our weaknesses for his glory—to not only change others but to transform us as well. Through the conflict, God gently exposed my friend's tendency to flee and hide, which is his refusal to be strong, and called him to be a warrior for his friend against the leader who was involved.

During the course of our conversation, my friend pointed out that, unlike him, I am far more ready for a fight, more open to conflict, and far less apt to hide. I told him of the situation God had put me in at that time, which was to not fight but to stand and see that the battle was God's, not mine. My friend reminded me of the passage in 2 Chronicles 20 where the warriors were told not to fight but to allow the choir to go before them and sing. As they sang, God routed the three armies that were about to destroy the people of God. God wanted me to avoid the fight; he wanted my friend to go to war.

In a similar way, we are each called by God to bring our strengths to the battle, and yet it is through our weaknesses that he intends to redeem us, our organizations, and our people (see 2 Corinthians 12:8–10). And when God redeems, it is his character that is made known through the transformation of our own character. There is no delight in life that is meant to be greater or sweeter than making known the heart of God through a humble and beautiful life. The effect is something remarkable on the inside and on the outside.

Remarkable on the Inside

Nothing is more thrilling than to see someone progress from simply following Christ to becoming a committed disciple. As the word *disciple* implies, there is a willingness, in this new role, not merely to hear and consider Christ's words but to submit to them and to take on his yoke as our own. It is the cry of Paul who says, "I want to know Christ and the power of his resurrection and the fellowship of sharing in his sufferings" (Philippians 3:10). In essence, he is saying, "I want power and I want intimacy." Paul is crying out for strength and tenderness—in different words, yet with the same desire to reveal God's good character. Transformation creates a deeper and more refined desire for the heart of God, the result of which will be greater gratitude, truth, and boldness.

Gratitude

If you're the worst of sinners, then you can relate personally to the words Jesus speaks to the woman in Luke 7: "But whoever has been forgiven little loves little" (v. 47 TNIV). That's because you know the other side of that equation is equally true: Whoever is forgiven much, loves much. And why, when you're the worst of sinners, do you love so much? Because you're so grateful!

In my experience, nothing chips away at gratitude more than the daily grind of leadership: the crises, confusion, conflicts, loneliness, and exhaustion. As leaders, we're sometimes amazed we're even able to get out of bed on certain mornings! We do, but do we do so with gratitude? Not the gratitude that comes when a problem is resolved, but gratitude that no matter how the issue plays out, we have the opportunity to be molded and shaped into a more glorious image of the person of Christ.

Gratitude deepens desire. The more grateful we are—the more our heart sings with the praise of beauty, goodness, and truth—the more we are seized by the small moments of grace that we "important" people are often too busy to see. It is true that the rich get richer. In this case, a wealth of gratitude sharpens our senses, making us increasingly able to take in the glories God has scattered throughout the world for us to find. No one is richer than those who are grateful.

Can you recall a significant battle you were called to fight years ago—one you presumed might destroy you? Do you recall the worry, the late nights, the strategic plans you made, and how it all went far worse than you could have dreamt in a nightmare? Did it burn away some of the dross? Did it mark you with scars worthy of revealing the suffering of Christ? In retrospect, do you bless that suffering and what it called you to become?

If not, then there may well be pockets of ingratitude—what we might typically call bitterness—that still reside in your heart. What you went through is still there, inviting you to look closely at your failure of tenderness or strength.

It is there to expose your habit of hiding or blaming. It is a window to help you look at your own struggle with lust and anger. In spite of all that has been left unaddressed, God has chosen to work through you and to bless you. Imagine how much many more opportunities he will have to do that once your heart is amazed that he calls you beloved and that you are known as fully as you can be known. It is time to allow fresh air to pour through those hidden places and to know forgiveness, wonder, and gratitude.

Truth

If I'm the worst of sinners and I know I have no right or reason by competence or knowledge to be the president of my organization—no more so than you do to be a pastor, a parent, or the owner of your business—then the reality is this: It is in our brokenness that we have our greatest opportunity to reveal the heart of God's goodness. Will we take that opportunity? Will we tell the truth?

If we tell the *truth*, here is the fundamental point: The worst is already known about us. What *worse* is there to know?

When we understand that the worst is already known, that offers us tremendous freedom to tell our stories and freedom, in our daily life, to reveal the character of God. Such conversations can take place on a plane. You can share your story as you interact over a cup of coffee.

The next time someone asks you, "What do you do for a living?" answer them: "I'm a storyteller with one story worth telling. Let me tell you about . . ."

Okay, you likely will never say those words, but there are a thousand ways of launching into your story that will make sense to the person, group, or audience you address. The next time someone complains to you about their spouse, their work, or their life, resist the urge to merely say, "Hey, me too." We can all do far, far better.

For starters, we can ask hard questions, but only if we are willing to answer those same questions ourselves. We can invite people to tell their stories as fully as they desire. We can inquire about matters that they only hint at but don't name, whether it involves work, or faith, or a personal issue. Doing so needn't take the form of barging in. Instead, begin by asking for permission: "Jack, you mentioned that things are not good with your wife. I'm not a marriage counselor, but I have known, and at times still know, great heartache with my wife. We also know great sweetness and hope. I don't want to blow off your remark about whether you two are going to make it, but I also don't know if I have permission to ask you more. Do you want me to step into these issues with you?"

Making such an offer may launch a process that will consume many hours (weeks, months) of your time. It may generate real sorrow and pain as you identify with your friend's situation. The payoff, however, can be great, because when combined with gratitude, truth will always birth greater boldness in our lives.

Boldness

The more grateful I am—when the worst is already known about me—then I am, indeed, free to fail. I'm free to take risks. Ultimately, I'm free to not worry, in one sense, about the consequences. I'm free to take the bold steps needed as a leader. I am free to make the difficult decisions required of me as a leader. I am free to reveal both my strength and my tenderness. Why? Because if everything is a gift, then, fundamentally, we need not fear loss.

A dear friend, in the middle of a contentious and highly politicized power struggle with his church board, took a bold and unexpected stand. For years, one elder had bullied the board to vote his way by threatening to quit the church and take with him the 20 percent of the church's finances contributed by his extended family.

Even my friend came under attack. That elder had vigorously opposed my friend's selection as senior pastor, but lost. In the job interview, my friend disclosed to the board that he had struggled with alcoholism in his earlier years. He had sought treatment and had over a decade of sobriety. If the board hired him, he didn't want them to later be surprised by this information.

Soon after, subtle and vicious rumors began. My friend endured the assaults. He addressed the accusations in public. He lived out what it means to love one's enemies. But in an effort to avoid conflict, he at times failed to speak his mind and vote in a manner consistent with his conscience.

After several years, the powerful elder again threatened to resign. This time the rest of the board gleefully accepted. My friend disagreed. He said if the elder were to resign, it should not be in that context. He then admitted that he too had become bitter and resentful, believing the elder was the basis for the rumor nightmare that he and his family had endured. Confessing that he was wrong, he asked for the elder's forgiveness.

The board was stunned. One elder said, "Until we deal with our own failure and learn to make decisions without the fear of his departure, we are no better."

The story doesn't have a smooth Christian sit-com ending. A few elders resigned. The powerful elder sneered at the cowards and remained on the board. But now, due to my friend's bold courage in a drama of repentance, new board members serve with a sense of integrity and joy, making decisions without the shadow of fear and regret.

The reality is that both the blessings and sorrows of this life are a gift. And if I am to welcome hardship as a friend and make a place for it in my heart to serve the greater purposes of God, then will I pray for boldness as the apostle Paul did? Paul prayed for boldness more often than he made any other request.

Will you pray for boldness in using your story? If you're a pastor with abuse in your past, will you use the story? Do you understand how many people in this world have never heard the words "sexual abuse" from a pulpit despite the fact that some 60 percent of women and in the range of 38 percent of men struggle with a history of such trauma? Why is that not being named? Are we aware there is spousal abuse in many congregations? Do we name that?

Do we own up to the fact that instead of dealing directly with someone at work, we go to someone else and gossip, conducting a guerrilla war against the person we dislike? Almost every work environment permits and utilizes collusion. We go to someone else to complain about a coworker. We don't speak directly to the coworker. And if someone is complaining to us about a coworker, we listen and then add a line or two about our own discontent. Collusion, like gossip, is a dark means of creating cohesion in subgroups, yet it can ruin an organization faster than a competitor's strategy to take away one's market share.

Can we name our darkness? Why should we? Because as people who have been there, we are the ones with the greatest sense of hope that redemption truly does redeem.

Indeed, then, if we're grateful, we can risk. And if we can risk, the promise is this: We will be more open and more honest. We will be freer. And the result of that, I believe, is that we'll become bolder, happier people. What an odd thing: Darkness leads to joy. Truth leads to a greater truth. Where have we heard this before?

Remarkable on the Outside

The bottom line, then, is this: If we want to be people who transform our worlds, it will begin when we describe the *character* of our story as an *absence of character* that's being redeemed by a *great character*, and that is the God of the universe. How do we begin? Let me tell you a story.

A friend asked if I would preach in his church. I said, "Yes, but why would you pay me to fly all the way across the country just to preach one time?" He explained that a conflict had arisen among his elders that he believed would be resolved only if they were willing to name their own failures before they addressed the weighty decision burdening them. "I want you to preach on owning up to being an adulterer and murderer from Matthew 5." I laughed. "You want to pay me to come in and tell the truth about myself so your elders might face what you are unable to say to them?" He laughed and admitted, "If I preached what you will say, I'd be in major trouble."

I was honored, but saddened. I told him I would do it, but for far more money than he had intended to pay, explaining that the wages of a "prophet" were simply higher than the pay of a preacher.

What is required to begin this truth-telling revolution? Like my friend who invited me to preach, we have to admit there is a problem, and the truth needs to be known and told. And that requires that we ask others to offer us the truth about ourselves and our organization.

Get Data That Is Irrefutable

I am amazed at how few organizations set aside the time and finances to take a good look at themselves. The best way I know to do this is through a review that surveys the organization from top to bottom, creating data the organization can use as part of its strategic planning and job evaluations. Unfortunately, one of the least-reviewed sectors in America is the local church. This, despite the fact that there are different groups that could provide valuable insights if they were surveyed, including the pastoral staff, administration, elders/deacons, lay leaders, volunteers, congregation, visitors, people who have come and left after a few visits, long-term involved attendees who have left unhappy, and others in the community who know of the church but don't attend. How do people perceive your work? Do those who serve understand your mission? Are attendees growing in their faith? It is impossible to make changes—or, at least, the right changes—and to measure your success if you don't know where you are right now.

Once you have the data, it is important to take sufficient time to digest it, personally and corporately, an activity in which a wise consultant can be a resource worth his or her weight in gold. Your consultant can offer a neutral, objective perspective and can assist you in not only digesting the information but in planning how best to communicate and implement the changes related to the findings.

You will also want to consider and digest what you learn elsewhere, including the information you read in this book. A word of caution: Don't read this material one week and decide to "go tell the truth" the next week, at the first opportunity to "get it off your chest." For your information to be effective, thoughtful preparation is required.

Get Data That Is Personal

To begin a major enterprise of data collection, reflection, and change requires a long-term strategy. To begin on a more limited basis, ask just three people who know you to give you feedback. How do you determine which people to ask? First, what three individuals do you trust? Let me assume one will be your spouse. (If it is not your spouse, then there are other issues that likely need to be addressed.) Second, pick a good friend unrelated to your work. And third, pick a trusted and confidential partner within your organization. Separately, ask all three these simple questions, to be answered in writing and returned to you before you meet. This builds on the work described earlier and takes a more personal look at your life.

- Describe for me a time when you felt: "I am so privileged to know you."

- Describe for me a situation when you thought: "He/she is so blind I can't believe it."

- In what situations would you assume I am most likely not going to tell the truth?

- In what moments do you feel most confident that I will rise to the occasion and handle a situation well?

Here is one way to use the data: give your trusted three people the questions, get their written feedback, meet with them one on one, ponder the data by journaling and praying, and then meet with the three of them together. Depending on the individuals involved and your receptivity to their feedback, this informal group may be as powerful and motivating as any consultant and as informative as the facts found in a more organized data-crunching process. Take the time and space to ponder what you have learned. Such a process might seem excessive, but if you are going to do this much work, then you might as well complete the whole marathon.

Allow Data about Your Dignity and Depravity to Amaze You

As you review the information, you will recognize a myriad of possibilities for change. But hold off on any actions until you have taken the time to be amazed—in awe of both your depravity and your dignity. We are meant to see the reality of our depravity as awe-full, provoking us to plead for mercy that is bountiful and free. We are also meant to experience the work of God in developing the goodness of our character as awe-some, prompting us to praise God.

Amazement is, in fact, better ground for transformation of character than mere action could ever be. Are you amazed? Are you humbled? I suspect both, and further, that you will be humbled because what you heard is as much about how wonderful it is to be in a relationship with you as how hard it is to deal with some elements of your character.

A simple rule of leadership is that we can never ask anyone to go any further than we are willing to go. If we labor for others' transformation of character, we must be the first to be transformed. If we want others to tell the truth, we must go first.

In the movie *We Were Soldiers Once . . . and Young*, Colonel Moore, the commanding officer, was the first boot to hit the battleground and, at the deeply moving end of the film, the last boot to leave the Vietnam battlefield where many of his men had died. During the height of the battle, someone back at headquarters demanded he leave the near certain massacre of his men. He refused and instead kept the promise he had made to be the first on the ground and the last to leave. He kept his word. Our task as leading characters is no different.

As a true leading character, my boot must strike the ground first and I must say, "This is a true saying, and everyone should believe it: Christ Jesus came into the world to save sinners—and I was the worst one of all" (see 1 Timothy 1:15). And I need to be the last boot off the ground, saying the same words, after the battle has ended.

When I am prone to quit, which seems far more often than is reasonable for a leading character, I find myself returning time and again to the last chapter in the last book Paul wrote before he was executed. He is in prison, cold and alone. And as he reflects on his life and the near certainty of his death, he says this:

> As for me, my life has already been poured out as an offering to God. The time of my death is near. I have fought a good fight, I have finished the race, and I have remained faithful. And now the prize awaits me—the crown of righteousness that the Lord, the righteous Judge, will give me on that great day of his return. And the prize is not just for me but for all who eagerly look forward to his glorious return.

> —2 Timothy 4:6–8, NLT

The day of death will come for each of us. And I know all of us long to be able to say we have fought the good fight, finished the race, and done so faithfully. Paul did so because he knew no one needed grace more than he did; no one was more in need of forgiveness. The prize for those who finish is the crown of righteousness that is summed up in the phrase, "Welcome home, my good and faithful servant."

Are you amazed? Are you humbled?

The more we allow our hearts to hear with strength and courage, tenderness and mercy, the more we will be amazed at how God has worked in us and longs to continue the good work he has begun.

We must be the first to say that we need transformation and the last to say it is finished. Such a leader I wish to become; such is a leader I'd follow to storm the gates of hell.

May that be true of all who lead with a true leading character.

Mars Hill Graduate School Conferences presents

THE LEADERSHIP CRUCIBL

WWW.LEADERSHIPCRUCIBLE.COM

WHAT IF YOU COULD
LEAD IN WAYS THAT ACTUALLY
MAKE A DIFFERENCE?

The Leadership Crucible is an innovative simulation experience that creates real-world leadership challenges and invites you to meet them. Taught by seasoned leaders Dan Allender and Ron Carucci, this imaginative, fictional leap into the crucible of everyday leadership makes a powerful connection between theory and praxis. In this two-and-a-half-day event, you will be:

- Challenged, stretched and encouraged

- Offered a safe context in which to risk, experiment and reflect

- Taught about the differences between incumbent and emergent leaders

- Provided feedback about how you make decisions, manage conflict, build consensus, and respond to changing demands

- Equipped to lead in ways that actually make a difference—in your work, your organization, your relationships, and yourself

EXPERIENCE LEADERSHIP & FAITH
IN A WHOLE NEW WAY

LEADERSHIP DEVELOPMENT MATTERS

The Leadership Summit, a two-day event, convenes every August in the Chicago area and is satellite broadcast live to more than 135 locations across North America. Designed for leaders in any arena—ministry, business, nonprofit—its purpose is to encourage and equip Christian leaders with an injection of vision, skill development, and inspiration.

When Leadership and Discipleship Collide

Bill Hybels

What do you do when the laws of leadership collide with the teachings of Christ?

Modern business practice and scholarship have honed the laws of leadership. To achieve success, you're supposed to—among other things—leverage your time, choose a strong team and avoid unnecessary controversy. But what happens when the laws of leadership and discipleship collide?

Using stories from his own life and ministry, Bill Hybels shows how the laws of leadership sometimes crash headlong into the demands of discipleship. And how the decisions you make at that point could affect not only you, but the destiny of those you lead.

Hardcover: 978-0-310-28306-5

Pick up a copy today at your favorite bookstore!

www.willowcreek.com

Making Vision Stick

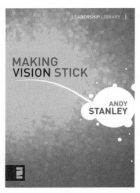

Andy Stanley

Vision is the lifeblood of your organization.

It should be coursing through the minds and hearts of those you lead, focusing their creativity and galvanizing their efforts. Together, you and your team will strive to make your vision a reality.

But in order for that to happen, you've got to make your vision stick. That's your responsibility as the leader.

Pastor and author Andy Stanley first shows you the reasons why vision doesn't stick. Then, sharing vivid firsthand examples, he walks you through five simple but powerful ways to make your vision infiltrate the hearts, minds, and lives of those you lead.

Making Vision Stick provides the keys you need to propel your organization forward.

Hardcover: 978-0-310-28305-8

Pick up a copy today at your favorite bookstore!

Overcoming Your Shadow Mission

John Ortberg

Do you lead from your mission. . . or your shadow mission?

A mission is the highest purpose to which God calls us; a shadow mission is an authentic mission that has been derailed. Every leader has a mission—and a shadow mission. Leaders must learn to name their shadow missions if they are ever to overcome them.

With characteristic humor and insight, Ortberg gives readers the tools to identify and combat the shadows that confront them and their organizations. From the story of a young Hebrew girl named Esther come the lessons that allow leaders to not only defeat their shadow mission, but to live out the authentic mission to which God calls them.

Hardcover: 978-0-310-28760-5

Pick up a copy today at your favorite bookstore!

www.willowcreek.com

This resource was created to serve you and to help you build a local church that prevails. It is just one of many ministry tools that are part of the Willow Creek Resources® line, published by the Willow Creek Association together with Zondervan.

The Willow Creek Association (WCA) was created in 1992 to serve a rapidly growing number of churches from across the denominational spectrum that are committed to helping unchurched people become fully-devoted followers of Christ. Membership in the WCA now numbers over 12,000 Member Churches worldwide from more than ninety denominations.

The Willow Creek Association links like-minded Christian leaders with each other and with strategic vision, training and resources in order to help them build prevailing churches designed to reach their redemptive potential. Here are some of the ways the WCA does that.

The Leadership Summit—A once a year, two-day learning experience to envision and equip Christians with leadership gifts and responsibilities. Presented live on Willow's campus as well as via satellite simulcast to over 135 locations across North America—plus more than eighty international cities feature the Summit by way of videocast every Fall—this event is designed to increase the leadership effectiveness of pastors, ministry staff, volunteer church leaders and Christians in the marketplace.